LUDLOW TO HEREFORD

including the Kington Branches

Vic Mitchell and Keith Smith

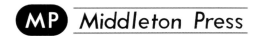
MP Middleton Press

Front cover: Kington was at the hub of four minor lines and two short trains were recorded there on 15th September 1949. The 6.0pm from Presteign is arriving behind 0-4-2T no. 5814 to connect with the 6.5pm from New Radnor to Leominster. (SLS coll.)

Back cover: The rear of the 08.45 Cardiff Central to Manchester Piccadilly is seen at Ludlow on 13th March 1995. Class 158 units were providing the most frequent service ever experienced on the route. (N.Sprinks)

**To commemorate 150 years
since the opening of
the branch line to Kington.**

Published September 2007

ISBN 978 1 906008 14 7

© Middleton Press, 2007

Design Deborah Esher
Typesetting Barbara Mitchell

Published by
> *Middleton Press*
> *Easebourne Lane*
> *Midhurst*
> *West Sussex*
> *GU29 9AZ*
Tel: 01730 813169
Fax: 01730 812601
Email: info@middletonpress.co.uk
www.middletonpress.co.uk

Printed & bound by Biddles Ltd, Kings Lynn

CONTENTS

1	Ludlow to Hereford	1 - 59
2	New Radnor Branch	60 - 108
3	Presteign Branch	109 - 120

INDEX

50	Barrs Court Junction	60	Kingsland	104	New Radnor
19	Berrington & Eye	84	Kington	65	Pembridge
42	Dinmore	23	Kington Junction	111	Presteign
100	Dolyhir	25	Leominster	49	Shelwick Junction
35	Ford Bridge	1	Ludlow	97	Stanner
109	Forge Crossing Halt	72	Marston Halt	75	Titley Junction
51	Hereford	45	Moreton-on-Lugg	8	Woofferton

ACKNOWLEDGEMENTS

We are very grateful for the assistance received from many of those mentioned in the credits also to D.Askew, W.R.Burton, A.R.Carder, R.Caston, L.Crosier, G.Croughton, M.Dart, A.Horner, P.Jones, N.Langridge, B.Lewis, Mr D. and Dr S.Salter, T.Ward and, in particular, our wives Barbara Mitchell and Janet Smith.

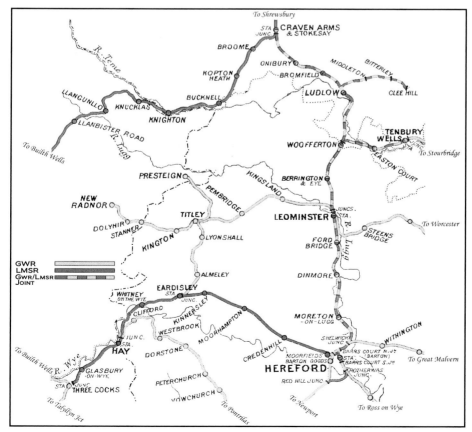

I.Railway Clearing House map of 1947.

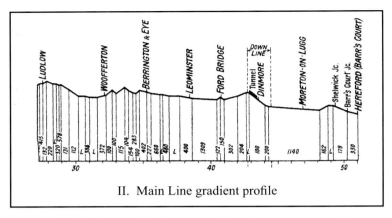

II. Main Line gradient profile

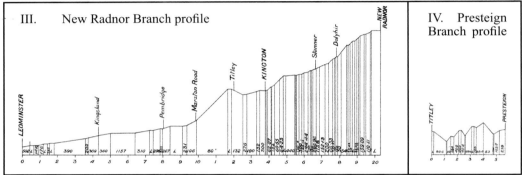

III.   New Radnor Branch profile

IV.   Presteign Branch profile

GEOGRAPHICAL SETTING

The route links three old-established market centres. Ludlow is situated on the River Teme, which flows south, close to the railway, as far as Woofferton, where it turns eastwards. In this vicinity, the line leaves Shropshire to enter the old county of Herefordshire and climbs over the watershed to the drainage area of the south-flowing River Lugg, which is encountered close to Leominster station.

This watercourse is followed to the outskirts of the county town of Hereford, except in the vicinity of Dinmore, where an extensive meander of over one mile eastwards necessitated tunnelling under the headland. Most of the line was built over Lower Old Red Sandstone, as were the branches. However, the terminal towns of both of these were on the upland area formed of Wenlock Limestone.

Presteigne is on the River Lugg, while Kington developed on the River Arrow, which joins the former close to Leominster and was in fairly close proximity to the branch. The final 3½ miles of the branch to New Radnor was in Radnorshire and thus in Wales. This also applied to the last ½ mile of the line to Presteigne, which was the county town, but it did not have a final "e" in the railway world and thus not elsewhere in this album.

The maps are to the scale of 25ins to 1 mile, with north at the top, unless otherwise indicated.

HISTORICAL BACKGROUND

Known as the "North and West Route", the Shrewsbury & Hereford Railway opened the section north of Ludlow on 21st April 1852 and the part south thereof on 6th December 1853. Trains ran to Newport from January 1854. The S&HR was initially single line throughout. It became the joint property of the London & North Western Railway, the Great Western Railway and the West Midland Railway on 1st July 1862. Track doubling followed in stages and the WMR became part of the GWR in August 1863.

An Act of 1871 confirmed the LNWR and GWR as joint owners of the S&HR. In the meantime, a broad gauge GWR line to Hereford from Ross had opened in 1855 and a standard gauge one from Malvern had come in 1861. The 1864 line from Hay eventually became a Midland Railway route. The complex links at Hereford are outlined later in this album. GWR trains began running between Woofferton and Tenbury Wells in 1861.

The branch from Leominster to Kington came into use on 20th August 1857, having been built under an Act of 10th July 1854 by the Leominster & Kington Railway Company. It was leased by the WMR from 1st July 1862 and subsequently by its successor, the GWR, with which it was amalgamated on 1st July 1898. The L&KR had opened the branch to Presteign from Titley Junction on 10th September 1875.

The Kington & Eardisley Railway received its Act on 30th June 1862 and the line south from Titley Junction was opened on 25th September 1875. This company also opened a remote section between Kington and New Radnor on the same day. Both lengths became part of the GWR, but the former section was closed between 1917 and 1922, succumbing permanently in 1940. It is featured in our *Branch Lines around Hay-on-Wye*.

The LNWR became part of the London Midland & Scottish Railway in 1923, but the GWR retained its identity. A joint operation of the North and West Route continued until nationalisation in 1948, when all lines in the area became part of the Western Region of British Railways.

Withdrawal of passenger services followed thus:

Kington - New Radnor	5th February 1951
Leominster - Bromyard	19th September 1952
Titley Jn. - Presteign	7th February 1955
Leominster - Kington	7th February 1955
Woofferton - Tenbury Wells	31st July 1961
Hereford - Hay-on-Wye	31st December 1962
Hereford - Ross-on-Wye	2nd November 1964

Cessation of freight traffic is detailed in the captions.

Privatisation in 1996 resulted in South Wales & West providing services ("South" was dropped in 1998). However, after reorganisation in 2001, Wales & Borders became the franchisee. Arriva Trains Wales took over in December 2003.

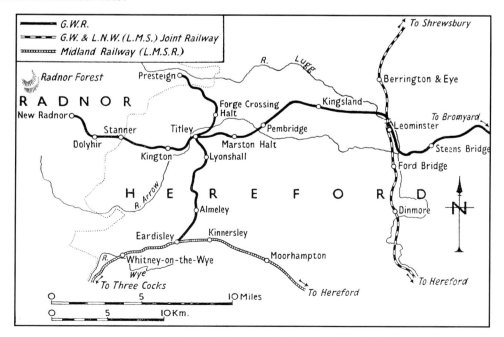

V. Branch lines to Kington. (Railway Magazine)

Kington Railway

The Hay Tramway from the Brecknock & Abergavenny Canal at Brecon had reached Hay on 7th May 1816, and was being completed to Eardisley. In the Autumn of 1817, a group of business-men in Kington decided to promote what was virtually an extension of this tramway from Eardisley to Kington and on to a lime works at Burlingjobb, 3½ miles west of the town, and the Act authorising this line, the Kington Railway, received the Royal Assent on 23rd May 1818.

The line followed a circuitous eight-mile route from Kington to Eardisley via Almeley and Lyonshall and was built to the same gauge of 3ft 6ins as the Hay Tramway, with which it connected. It was opened from Eardisley to Flood Gates, Kington, on 1st May 1820, with an opening ceremony being held on 18th May 1820.

There is no record of the date of opening the last 3½ miles to Burlingjobb, though it was still unfinished in May 1833, but must have opened soon after. Clients using the line paid tolls and conveyed their merchandise in their own wagons, drawn by their own teams of horses.

In 1862, the Kington Railway was acquired by the newly-promoted Kington & Eardisley Railway, which was opened on 3rd August 1874. However, the new railway company kept running the 3ft 6ins gauge tramway from Sunset Wharf, Kington, to Burlingjobb, despite the complication of having to tranship goods at Kington. Eventually this section was replaced by a regular railway, which became part of the Kington & Eardisley's line from Kington to New Radnor.

PASSENGER SERVICES

Down trains are southbound and those running on at least five days per week are described below, with the Sunday frequency shown in brackets. Initially, Ludlow received four trains from Shrewsbury and there were seven (2) to Hereford for most of the 1860s, although only three (1) stopped at all stations south of Leominster. By 1878, there were an additional four fast trains on weekdays.

Hereford was receiving 11 (4) trains from the north in 1890, but most small stations were only served by four (1) of them. There were an extra two south to Leominster at this time.

By 1910, 15 (4) southbound trains were arriving at Hereford, two of them having started at Ludlow. There were also two shorter workings, but the smaller stations had only four or five (0) calling.

The table left indicates the number of trains calling at Ludlow, Leominster and Hereford. In brackets are the all-station services.

The sample timetables for the Kington Branches (right) give the best indication of the evolution of services. It is important to note that trains to Presteign and Eardisley originated at Kington and not Titley Junction.

	Weekdays	Sundays
1930	10 (7)	3 (0)
1950	9 (4)	3 (0)
1970	6	2 *
1990	14 *	4
2007	26 *	10 *

* Not all trains called at Leominster.

SHREWSBURY and HEREFORD.—In connection with London and North Western and Great Western.

June 1869

STEENS BRIDGE, LEOMINSTER, KINGTON, NEW RADNOR, and PRESTEIGN LINES.—G.W.

Down.	mrn	gov	aft	aft	aft	gov	aft	aft		Up.	mrn	aft	aft	aft	aft	gov	aft		mdl
Steens Bridge dep	9 20	1230	3 45				8 0			Presteign dep	7 25	11 0	2 35		5 5	5 0	7 10		mrn aft
Leominster 215	30	9 55	1 5	4 20	5 55		8 35			Titley { below	7 39	11 14	2 39		6	5 47	7 24		
Kingsland 214	5 50	10 5	1 15	4 31	6 8		8 45			Kington arr	7 45	1130	2 50		6	6 57	7 30		
Pembridge	6 10	1012	1 22	4 39	6 19		8 53												
Titley (below)	6 30	1023	1 33	4 52	6 35		9 5			— New Radnor d		1055		2 15	6 0				
Kington	6 35	1027	1 37	4 57	6 40		9 10			2¼ Dolyhir	11 1			2 22	6 6				
Stanner		1039	1 57	5 15						3⅓ Stanner	11 6			2 27	6 11				
Dolyhir		1044	2 3	5 24						Kington	7 55	1115		2 40	6 25		7 40		8 0
New Radnor		1050	2 9	5 30						Titley	8 0	1120		2 45	6 33		7 45		8 7
Kington arr	6 45	1030	1 25		5 0	6 45				Pembridge	8 10	1131		2 55	6 45		7 55		8 19
Titley { arr	6 50	1034	1 30		5 4	6 49				Titley	8 14	1140		3 4	6 53		8 5		8 10
{ dep	6 55	1035	1 35		5 5	6 50				Kingsland	458	19	1140		3 157	2	8 15		8 20
Presteign arr	7 10	1050	1 50		5 20	7 5				Steens Bridge a	9 10	1220		3 387	40				

February 1890

LEOMINSTER, KINGTON, and NEW RADNOR.—Great Western.

KINGTON and EARDISLEY.—Great Western.

KINGTON and PRESTEIGN.—Great Western.

July 1910

LEOMINSTER, KINGTON, and NEW RADNOR.

KINGTON, EARDISLEY, and PRESTEIGN.

November 1930

Table 176 — LEOMINSTER, TITLEY, KINGTON, and NEW RADNOR

Table 177 — KINGTON, TITLEY, and PRESTEIGN

June 1950

Table 176 — LEOMINSTER, TITLEY, and KINGTON (Third Class only)

	Miles		Week Days only								Miles		Week Day only			
			a.m a.m		p.m p.m		p.m						a.m a.m		p.m p.m	
Leominster dep			6 18 9 50		1235 4 55		8 25				Kington dep			7 20 11 7		1 50 7 5	
4¼ Kingsland			6 29 9 59		1250 5 4		8 34				1½ Titley			7 25 1112		1 55 7 9	
8 Pembridge			6 38 10 7		1 2 5 14		8 41				5½ Marston Halt			7 30 1118		2 5 7 14	
10 Marston Halt			6 44 1012		1 9 5 17		8 47				8 Pembridge			7 37 1124		2 1 7 20	
12 Titley			6 52 1020		1 17 5 24		8 52				12 Kingsland			7 46 1133		2 21 7 29	
13½ Kington arr			6 57 1024		1 24 5 29		8 57				13½ Leominster arr			7 55 1140		2 21 7 36	

S Saturdays only.

December 1953

1. Ludlow to Hereford

LUDLOW

VI.   The 1928 edition at 6 ins to 1 mile has the Clee Hill freight-only branch curving at the top. It was in use in 1864-1962. The engine shed closed in December 1951.

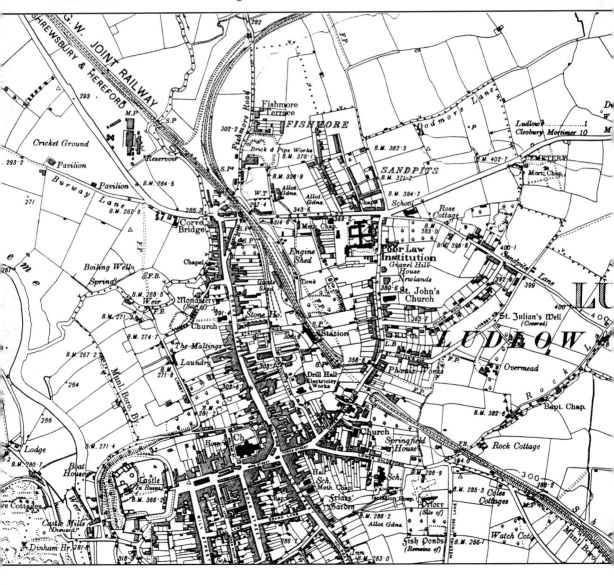

1.   This southward view is from 1923 and has the mouth of the 132yd. long tunnel in the distance. The ridge of high ground bears the church and castle, further west. The crossing in the foreground was for staff use only. (Stations UK)

2.   The curvature made a footbridge a highly desirable feature and necessitated the banner repeater signal by the tunnel mouth. Gas lights were still in evidence in September 1960. (H.C.Casserley)

3.	A July 1961 panorama includes the goods yard, which closed on 6th May 1968, and the 1935 signal box (centre), which had 62 levers and closed on 5th June 1968. There had been two boxes previously, North and Station. (R.G.Nelson/T.Walsh)

4.   The LCGB "Welsh Borderer" railtour was hauled by ex-LMS "Jubilee" class 4-6-0 no. 5596 *Bahamas* of 1935 on 14th October 1972. The locomotive was based at the Dinting Railway Centre for many years and stopped here for prolonged photography. (B.I.Natham)

5.   The station had served 4552 residents in 1901 and 6800 in 1961. The west elevation is seen three years later. Demolition soon followed.
(Lens of Sutton coll.)

6.   A survey of the scene in September 1999 reveals a small cabin serving as a ticket office, the original structures having been demolished in the late 1960s. The tasteful new waiting shelter is in contrast. (B.W.L.Brooksbank)

7.   No. 158822 was working a northbound service on 18th March 2004. The fresh new building housed Ludlow Station Travel, which issued tickets and had a bookstall. (M.Turvey)

WOOFFERTON

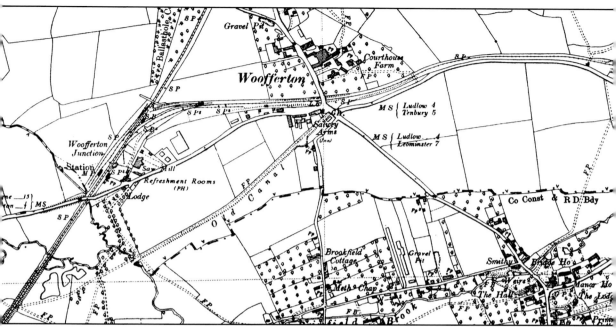

VII.   The line from Ludlow is at the top. There had been an intermediate station at Ashford Bowdler between about December 1854 and November 1855. There was a 19-lever signal box at the level crossing there until the 1930s, but since 1973 there has been an automatic half-barrier level crossing at its site. On the right of this 1952 map at 6ins to 1 mile is the branch to Tenbury Wells, which carried passengers from 1861 to 1961. The village of Woofferton housed 154 souls in 1901.

8.   A northward view recorded during shunting in about 1923 includes the loop used by branch trains, but its short bay platform is obscured by the building on the left. (Lens of Sutton coll.)

9.   The 11.10am Hereford to Shrewsbury was hauled by 4-6-0 no. 7023 *Penrice Castle* on 10th September 1949. The train called at all stations and the 50¾ mile journey took 2hrs 1min. (H.C.Casserley)

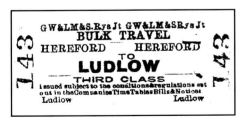

10.	A panorama from the Winter of 1953-54 shows the branch loop more clearly, but empty flower beds, contrasting with other views of fine floral displays. (P.J.Garland/R.S.Carpenter coll.)

11.	The branch train is signalled for the up main line. There was a service for school pupils between Tenbury Wells and Ludlow. Also evident on 17th July 1959 is the shunt signal on the down platform. (H.C.Casserley)

12.   The branch engine shed is seen in 1959. Although it had closed in November 1896, it was still standing as it supported the water tank. (R.S.Carpenter)

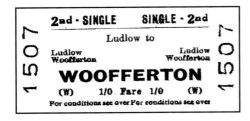

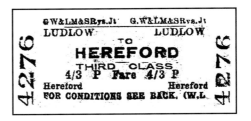

13.   The nameboard and a lamp post stand on the bay platform in this 1961 photograph. It was in use until 1957 and there had been a direct connection to the branch between it and the tank wagon. (R.G.Nelson/T.Walsh)

14.   There was obvious provision for gentlemen on both platforms, but no other signs are evident. The picture was taken shortly before closure on 31st July 1961. However, goods facilities remained until 7th October 1963. (J.Moss/R.S.Carpenter coll.)

15.   Running north on 1st October 1976 is no. 47157; the goods shed and signal box are in the background. Each side are the goods loops, which were added in 1941. The down one became a siding in 1961 and was lost in 1985. (T.Heavyside)

16.   Three photographs from 10th May 1989 show details which had changed little 18 years later. The 1889 box had been between the branch and the main line and there had been a ballast pit siding on the left from 1876 into the 20th century. (P.G.Barnes)

17.   In addition to the up goods loop, the box controlled two crossovers. The pin-ups include many diesels. A frame with 75 levers was installed in 1914, but this was reduced to 39 in 1964. (P.G.Barnes)

18.   The north end of the loop is included in the picture of no. 37886 passing with rolls of steel from Scotland, bound for South Wales. (P.G.Barnes)

BERRINGTON & EYE

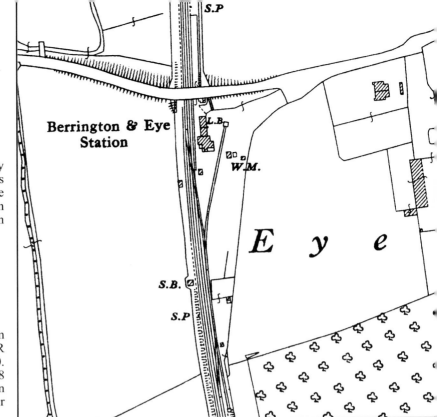

Berrington & Eye Station

E y e

VIII. The 1928 survey indicates orchards nearby and also that Eye was close. Its population dropped from 315 in 1901 to 192 in 1961.

19. Running in from the north is a LNWR 2-4-0 in about 1900. Berrington housed 928 in 1901. The down platform continued under the bridge. (Postcard)

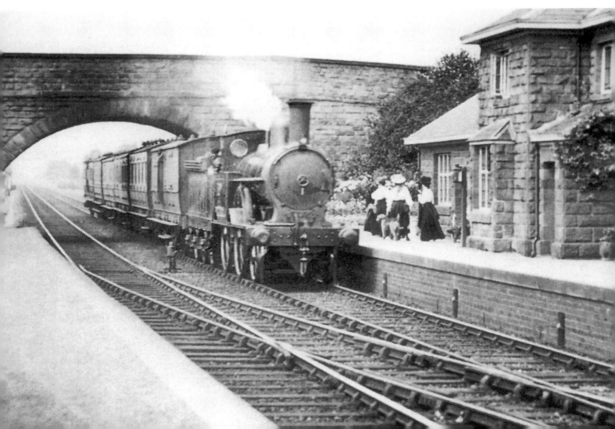

20.   A southerly panorama from about 1930 includes the 4½ ton capacity crane and the 1875 signal box. This remained in use until about 1957, its 1907 frame having 19 levers. (Mowat coll./Brunel University)

21.   The steps up to the road from the up platform are included in this photograph from about 1935, as is the full length of the down platform. (Stations UK)

22.   Passenger service was withdrawn on 9th June 1958 and goods followed on 4th January 1960. This is the scene a few years later. Kington Junction was a little over three miles to the south. (Lens of Sutton coll.)

KINGTON JUNCTION

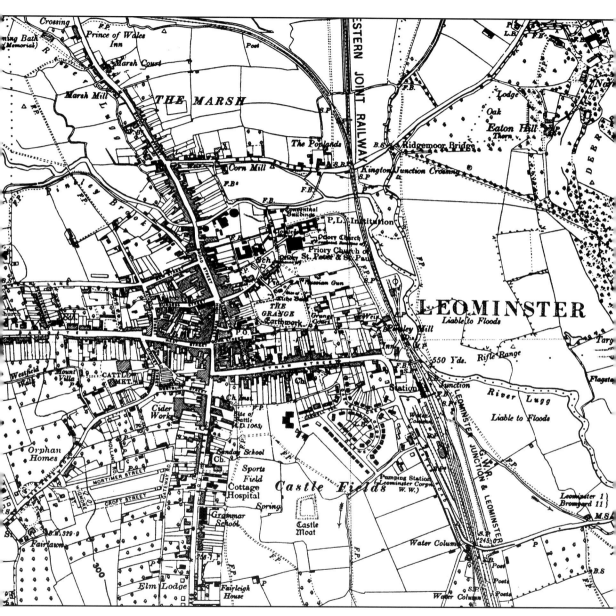

IX.   Kington Junction is shown near the top of this 1938 extract at 6 ins to 1 mile, the single line branch curving westwards. The LJ&L name at the bottom refers to the GWR-owned third track, which diverged after a mile or so to turn east to Bromyard and Worcester.

23.   Northbound over Kington Junction Crossing on 8th April 1946 is LMS 4-6-0 no. 5292. The location was renamed Leominster Crossing in April 1970, automatic half barriers having been installed in October 1966. (E.Johnson)

24.   The staff is surrendered as ex-GWR 0-4-2T leaves the Kington branch on 13th June 1964. All traffic ceased on it three months later. The signal box was called Kington Junction and functioned until 16th October 1966. It had a gate wheel and 21 levers. (P.J.Garland/R.S.Carpenter coll.)

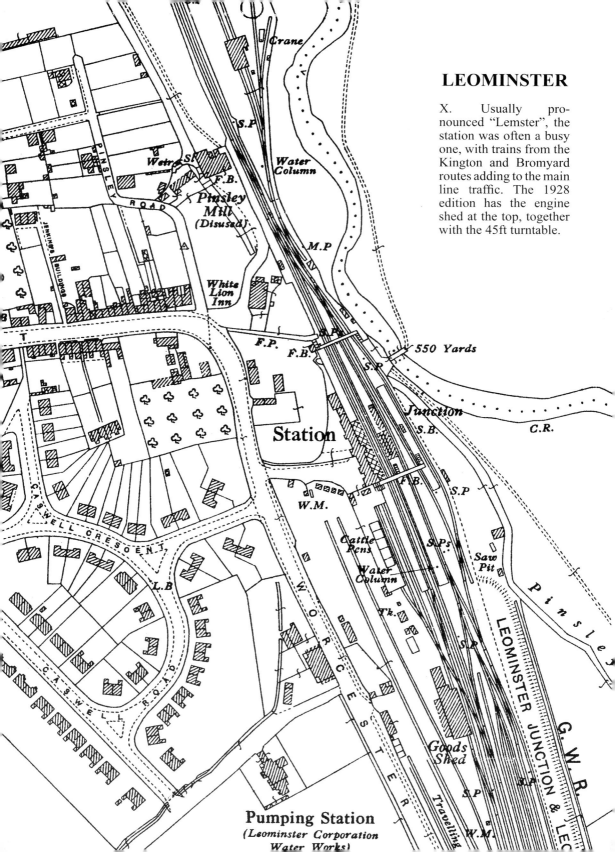

LEOMINSTER

X. Usually pro-nounced "Lemster", the station was often a busy one, with trains from the Kington and Bromyard routes adding to the main line traffic. The 1928 edition has the engine shed at the top, together with the 45ft turntable.

Crane

S.P.

Water Column

Weir St.

F.B.

Pinsley Mill (Disused)

PINSLEY ROAD

JENKINGS BUILDINGS

White Lion Inn

M.P

F.P.

F.B.

M.P

550 Yards

S.P

Junction
S.B.

C.R.

Station

F.B.

S.P

W.M.

S.Ps

Saw Pit

Cattle Pens

Water Column

Tk.

S.P

CASWELL CRESCENT

L.B

WORCESTER ROAD

CASWELL ROAD

LEOMINSTER JUNCTION & LEO

Pinsley

G.W.R.

Goods Shed

S.P

Travelling W.M.

S.P

Pumping Station
(Leominster Corporation
Water Works)

25.   Five platforms were available from 1897, three having for long brought operational limitations. This active scene was recorded on 7th May 1948, as ex-LMS 4-6-0 no. 4764 waits to leave for Hereford and ex-GWR 0-6-0PT no. 7416 is bound for Worcester. (R.G.Nelson/T.Walsh)

26.   This 1954 view from the footbridge emphasises the massive water requirement at a junction such as this. Fortunately the river was close by. Numerous mailbags await the up train. (Stations UK)

27.   The engine shed was used mostly by branch engines and is seen on 4th November 1956, with no. 4600 inside and no. 1445 outside. The shed was in use from 1901 until 30th April 1962. The chimney was on the sand drier and the crane was for coaling. The shed had been south of the station in the 19th century. (L.W.Perkins/F.A.Wycherley)

28.   Class 4800 0-4-2T no. 1455 waits with an autocoach for Tenbury Wells on 22nd August 1959. The pair had earlier worked a Ludlow-Craven Arms trip. The island platform on the left was added in 1884, when the first section of the Bromyard line opened. This platform was little used in later years. (Transport Treasury)

29.   A similar formation is seen at the same location on 3rd June 1961 and we can marvel at the unusual structure created in 1901 to support the Leominster Station box, which was in use until 31st May 1964. It had a massive frame containing 99 levers. Some trains ran between New Radnor and Worcester, but these were usually hauled by tender engines in the 1930s. (G.Adams/M.J.Stretton coll.)

30.   The other side of the massive box was recorded on the same day, as one of the new style of main line trains arrives. DMUs of this type began to appear in 1958, but the stylish cats whiskers would not last much longer. (G.Adams/M.J.Stretton coll.)

Other views of this station can be found in our *Worcester to Hereford* album, as it includes the Bromyard route.

31.	A view north on 13th August 1963 from the bridge featured on map XI includes the goods shed and 0-4-2T no. 1420. Goods traffic here ceased on 2nd January 1967. (B.W.L.Brooksbank)

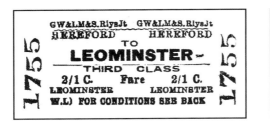

GW&LM&S.RlysJt   GW&LM&S.RlysJt
HEREFORD   HEREFORD
TO
LEOMINSTER
THIRD CLASS
2/1 C.   Fare   2/1 C.
LEOMINSTER   LEOMINSTER
W.L)   FOR CONDITIONS SEE BACK

1755   1755

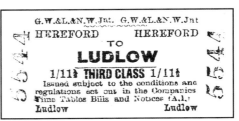

G.W.&L.&N.W.Jnt. G.W.&L.&N.W.Jnt
HEREFORD   HEREFORD
TO
LUDLOW
1/11½ THIRD CLASS 1/11½
Issued subject to the conditions and
regulations set out in the Companies
Time Tables Bills and Notices (A.L.)
Ludlow   Ludlow

5544   5544

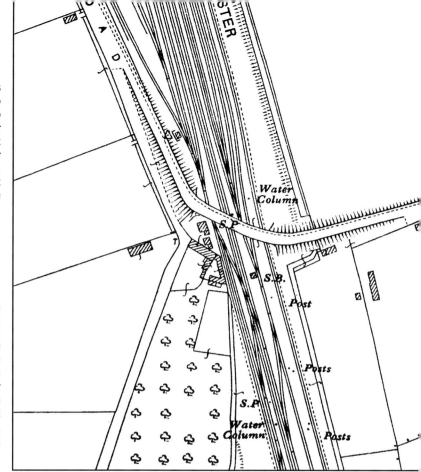

XI. The lengthy goods yard extended south onto this continuation of map X. Centre is Leominster South End signal box. It was known as Leominster Goods Yard at one period. The yard had no crane, but there was a 30cwt one in the goods shed.

32. South End box was renamed as shown when Station box was closed. Photographed in 2001, the 1875 box was still in use in 2007. It had new frames in 1902 and 1941; the latter one had 30 levers. The Bromyard line ran behind it until traffic ceased in 1952, after which time it was used for wagon storage.
(Ted Hancock Books)

33.   Two photographs from 22nd March 2004 reveal that much had survived, although only two running lines remained. There were two crossovers near the signal box, plus two sidings on the up side. No. 158831 is destined for Crewe. (M.Turvey)

34.   The building had been well conserved, although with few chimney pots. The Leominster District Council had saved it in 1983 by leasing it and then letting it out for commercial purposes. (M.Turvey)

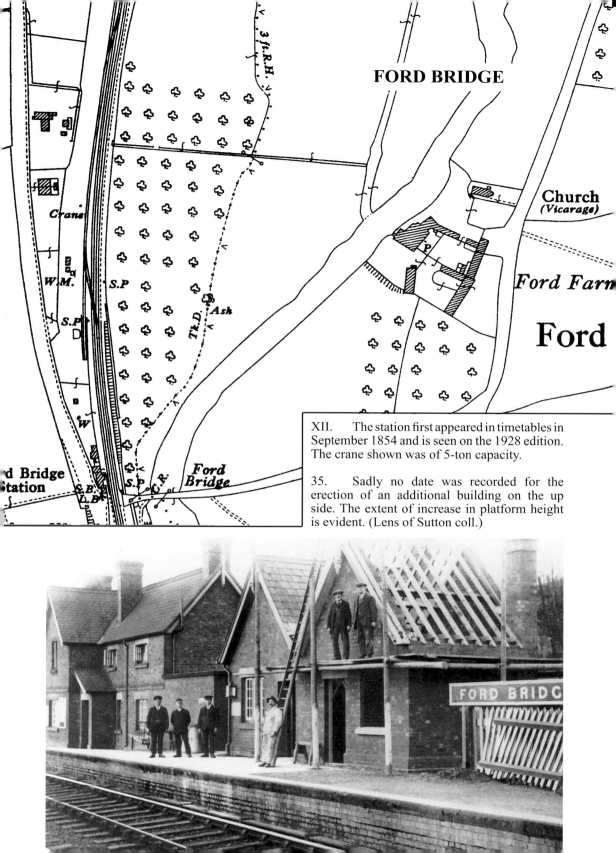

FORD BRIDGE

Church
(Vicarage)

Ford Farm

Ford

Crane

W.M.

S.P

S.P
D

Ash

Tk.D.

3ft.R.H.

S.P

W

d Bridge
tation

S.B.
L.B.

S.P

Ford
Bridge

XII.   The station first appeared in timetables in September 1854 and is seen on the 1928 edition. The crane shown was of 5-ton capacity.

35.   Sadly no date was recorded for the erection of an additional building on the up side. The extent of increase in platform height is evident. (Lens of Sutton coll.)

FORD BRIDG

36.	A view from the 1930s looking south includes all the passenger facilities. There was never a footbridge, but travellers crossed the tracks under the caring eyes of the signalman. (Stations UK)

37.	In the distance in this 1950s photograph is the connection to the goods yard, which was opened in 1890. The oil lighting was never modernised. One of Cadbury's factories was nearby and much milk was received by rail for it. (Lens of Sutton coll.)

38.   Goods and passenger services were withdrawn on 5th April 1954, but most buildings remained and are seen in the 1960s. The gates were wheel operated. Note that the track had been modernised. (Lens of Sutton coll.)

39.   The 1964 view includes the lamp hut, where the oil was kept and the wicks were trimmed. The gates were replaced by full lifting barriers on 24th September 1975 and the signalbox remained in use until 3rd October 1988. It had a 19-lever frame. (Stations UK)

40.   Based at Hereford, no. 6000 *King George V* worked a special from Shrewsbury to Newport on 3rd July 1977. It is entering the original 1852 tunnel; the second one was not completed until 1893. (T.Heavyside)

41.   Emerging from the earlier tunnel on 1st October 1976 is no. 47189 with southbound coal.
This bore was lined with 3.25m bricks. The later tunnel was built at a lower level at its north end
and on a gradient of 1 in 135. (T.Heavyside)

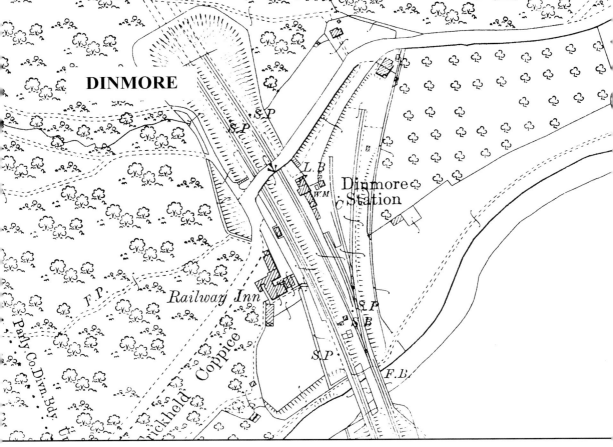

DINMORE

Railway Inn

XIII.   The station was at the southern end of the tunnels and the village recorded a population of 27 in 1901. (The map is from 1904.) However, freight was important and a crane of 4-ton capacity was provided.

42.   Passenger service was discontinued on 9th June 1958, but freight lasted until 1st June 1964. The signal box had been between the tracks and served as a ground frame between those dates. It had 15 levers. A northward view from about 1912 includes the high level platform and shelter on the left. (A.Dudman coll.)

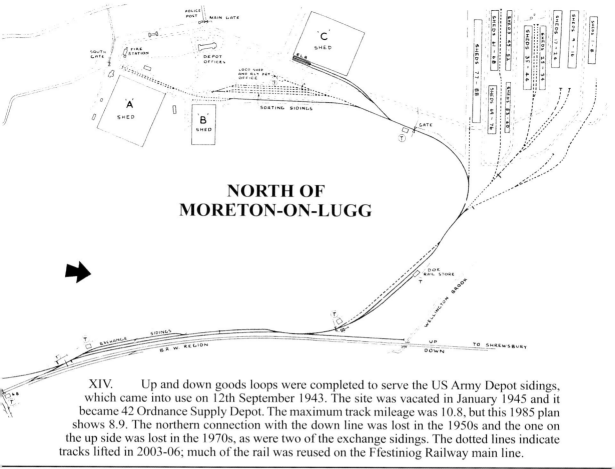

NORTH OF
MORETON-ON-LUGG

XIV. Up and down goods loops were completed to serve the US Army Depot sidings, which came into use on 12th September 1943. The site was vacated in January 1945 and it became 42 Ordnance Supply Depot. The maximum track mileage was 10.8, but this 1985 plan shows 8.9. The northern connection with the down line was lost in the 1950s and the one on the up side was lost in the 1970s, as were two of the exchange sidings. The dotted lines indicate tracks lifted in 2003-06; much of the rail was reused on the Ffestiniog Railway main line.

43. US Army Quartermaster Depot G-22 was photographed on 25th April 1944 as coils of communication cable were being prepared in readiness for D-Day. One of the lines shown lower right on the map is lower left here. (US National Archive)

44.   Army use ceased in 2000 and the site was sold for commercial use and gravel extraction.
Tarmac undertook the latter from 2004, after the track had been simplified, and three or four 1000-
ton trains left for Hayes, near Southall, each week. In 2007, one siding was used by the D2578
Locomotive Group to accommodate two preserved diesels. The site does not have public access.
The first loaded stone train is being drawn over the weighbridge by nos. 66121 on 16th June 2004
and it is passing the ex-Army engine shed, near which are no. D2578 and no. 03145. (N.Aitken)

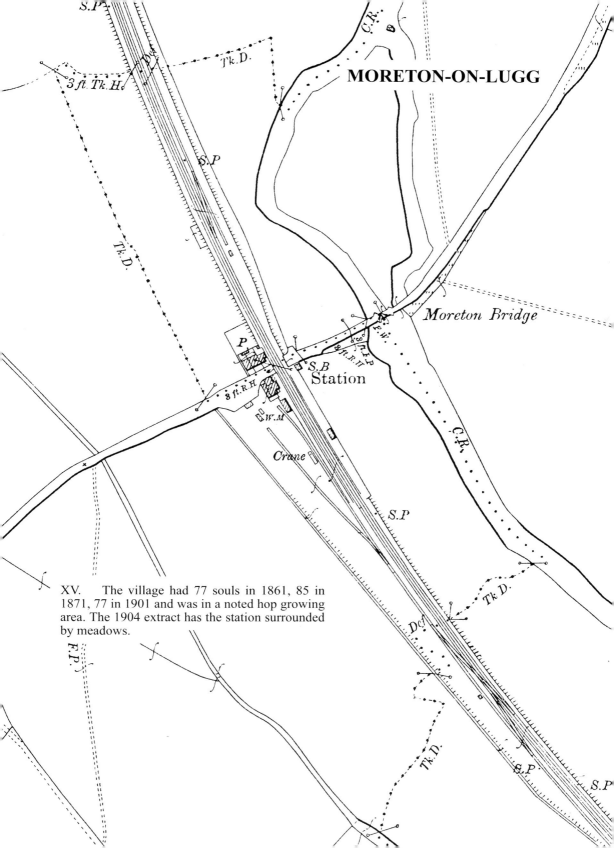

MORETON-ON-LUGG

S.P.

Tk.D.

3 ft. Tk. H.

Tk.D.

C.R.

Moreton Bridge

P

S.B

3 ft. R. P.

F.W.

Station

3 ft. R. H.

W.M

Crane

C.R.

S.P.

Tk. D.

XV.   The village had 77 souls in 1861, 85 in 1871, 77 in 1901 and was in a noted hop growing area. The 1904 extract has the station surrounded by meadows.

F.P.

D

Tk. D.

S.P.

S.P.

45.   This northward panorama was created a few weeks before passenger services were withdrawn on 9th June 1958. The first ticket office was reputed to be in a hollow oak tree and tea was served in another. (R.M.Casserley)

46.   A view from almost the same location on 20th November 1963 includes part of the crane, which was rated at one ton. Tank wagons containing water were provided at some stations devoid of mains supply. The original signal box had 20 levers and a new one was opened in 1943 to serve the enlarged layout, with a 44 lever frame. (R.G.Nelson/T.Walsh)

47.   A northbound Warship is about to obscure the crane shortly before the goods yard was closed on 28th September 1964. The right signal arm was for the Depot lines. Full lifting barriers came into use on 24th October 1975. (Stations UK)

48.   The same signals are seen again on 8th May 1989 as no. 37426 works the 15.00 Cardiff to Rhyl service. The points to the military complex are in the foreground. (P.G.Barnes)

49.   The signal box roof is above the second coach of this southbound special, hauled by ex-GWR 4-6-0 no. 6000 *King George V* on 15th February 1981. The double track to Worcester begins near the sixth coach. The locomotive received the bell while touring the USA in 1927. The signal box was closed when the Worcester route was singled on 20th October 1984. (J.Petley)

BARRS COURT JUNCTION

50.   The location can be found near the top of the next map. Our journey continues to the left, to the present Hereford station, for long known as Barrs Court. The 1878 signal box was in use until 31st July 1966. In the far background is Hereford Gasworks and nearer is the pylon works of Painter Bros. Both were served by sidings for more than 20 years after this photograph was taken in 1956. (P.J.Garland/R.S.Carpenter coll.)

HEREFORD

XVI. The remainder of our journey is on the curve on the top right quarter of this 1952 6 ins scale map. This section had for a long time been a joint LNWR/GWR operation, as had the station. It was known as Barrs Court until 1893, when the GWR's Barton station (lower left) closed. The latter was in use for freight until 1979. North of it was the MR's Moorfields terminus for trains from Brecon, but these ran to Barrs Court from 1893, via a new curve of small radius. This was still in place in 2004, serving a power station, two industrial premises and Bulmer's cider works. The MR engine shed is marked, although this had not been used since 1924. The straight route on the left carried through freight trains between the Midlands and South Wales until 1966. The Bulmer Railway Centre (1968-93) was near the triangle on the left and is featured in pictures 11-13 in our *Branch Lines around Hay-on-Wye*.

51. Our journey ends at the island platform, seen here in about 1923. Trains from Gloucester via Ross had been broad gauge until 1869 and a separate engine shed was provided behind the camera. It was later used as a carriage shed, the main loco depot being established at Barton. On the right is the eastern goods shed. A pair had been erected by the joint operating companies. There was a staff of 172 at this time. (Chambers coll./HMRS)

52. The left signal arms in this northward view from 1937 are for trains taking the Brecon Curve, on their way to Hay-on-Wye. The engine shed housed LNWR engines until 1923 and LMS ones until its closure in 1938. It is marked above the centre of the map and the GWR loco sheds are lower left. (D.K.Jones coll.)

53.	This is the south end of the up platform, again in the 1920s. The two through roads were then used mainly for carriage berthing, as through freight trains mostly ran on the direct Barton route. (Stations UK)

54.	This northward panorama is from 28th March 1937 and it includes the signal box, known as Ayleston Hill until 8th June 1983. It has since been the only box in the area and has sixty levers and a panel. (D.K.Jones coll.)

55.   The 10.05 Birmingham Snow Hill to Cardiff snakes over the points on 20th August 1963; the second coach had a mini-buffet. Above it can be seen part of the former GWR goods shed. It survives in commercial use, but the other was demolished. (B.S.Jennings)

56.   The first permanent station on this site was completed in 1855 and was replaced by this fine structure during major improvements in 1878-83. The first station had a large shed containing bay platforms end to end nearest the building and a through line on the east side. The latter was mixed gauge, the southern bay was broad and the northern one standard. This is a 1973 photograph. (J.C.Gillham)

57.   We can now enjoy two views from the bridge north of the station on 14th August 1984. First we look south and see both goods sheds out of use and the up platforms, plus bay, between them. The DMU is working the 18.45 service to London. (D.H.Mitchell)

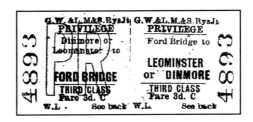

67. We now have four photographs from about 1957. The signal box near the gates was in use from November 1926 until August 1958. It had 12 levers and was transplanted from Kilkelwydd. Gleaming on the left is a Morris Minor Estate. (J.Moss/R.S.Carpenter coll.)

68. The weigh office (missing in our Kingsland survey) is on the left, as is the 6-ton crane. The goods shed accommodated wagons, unlike the one at Kingsland.
(J.Moss/R.S.Carpenter coll.)

69.   The full extent of the loop is clear; this signal box functioned between 1901 and 1926. The loop had been added in about 1880. Closure dates were as at Kingsland. (J.Moss/R.S.Carpenter coll.)

70.   This is almost a continuation of picture no. 67, which only shows the station house. The ticket office entrance was below the left chimney stack. (J.Moss/R.S.Carpenter coll.)

71.   The entire north elevation is seen in April 1963, by which time the signal box had been demolished. The ticket office had been at the far end. (P.J.Garland/R.S.Carpenter coll.)

MARSTON HALT

72.   Marston Lane Siding was reached about 100yds before the halt, which was on the other side of the level crossing in this westward view from June 1964. (P.J.Garland/R.S.Carpenter coll.)

73.   Here we look from the halt to the opposite side of the crossing cottage. There had been a station in this vicinity for 12 months from January 1863. (R.M.Casserley)

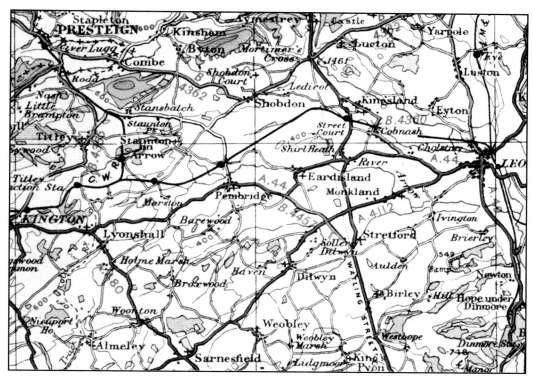

XIX.   The 1947 edition at 2 ins to 1 mile indicates the position of this halt and also Forge Crossing Halt, on the Presteign Branch.

74.   The halt opened on 26th April 1929 and it was situated ½ mile north of the village. It was built on or close to the site of the earlier station. (J.Peden/Stations UK)

TITLEY JUNCTION

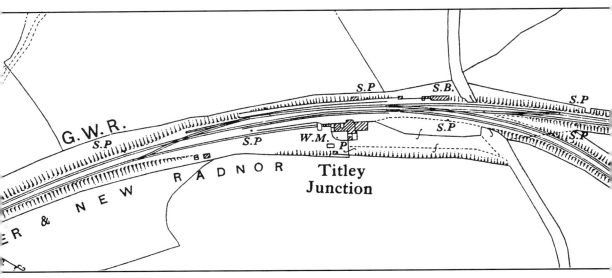

XX.   The 1928 edition has the converging tracks of the single line south to Eardisley on the right, lower. Above it are the two single lines from Leominster and from Presteign, which ran parallel to one another for one mile.

75.   An April 1932 eastward view includes the small goods shed on the right. There was a staff of seven here in 1903, but five sufficed for most of the 1930s. (Mowat coll./Brunel University)

Titley	1903	1913	1923	1933
Passenger tickets issued	11811	9951	7575	5179
Season tickets issued	*	*	12	-
Parcels forwarded	2263	2261	2015	2179
General goods forwarded (tons)	32	47	54	309
Coal and coke received (tons)	182	228	134	40
Other minerals received (tons)	125	700	84	666
General goods received (tons)	147	198	148	130
Trucks of livestock handled	25	61	12	12

(* not available)

76.   The two single lines with their separate signals are in the centre and the Eardisley lines are on the right. They join behind the notice board. There were five employees here for most of the 1930s. (Mowat coll./Brunel University)

77.   There were good connections here in the 1930s: a train from Leominster would arrive as one for Presteign waited in the adjacent platform. The latter services all originated at Kington. This peaceful view is from the signal box in 1935. (Stations UK)

78.   Branch motive power on 27th April 1947 was 0-4-2T no. 3574, still devoid of a full cab. The station water store is on the right. One train had served both Presteign and Eardisley in the 1930s. (R.S.Buckley/M.J.Stretton coll.)

79.   The special train on 27th July 1957 called for a rare opportunity to examine the premises, crutches or not. Lower right is evidence of the Eardisley branch, last used in 1940. (R.M.Casserley)

80.   A westward view from about 1959 includes the headshunt and loading gauge, plus one of the wooden coal wagons extended for the carriage of coke. (J.Moss/R.S.Carpenter coll.)

Other views can be seen in pictures 33-35 in our *Branch Lines around Hay-on-Wye*, which includes the line from Eardisley.

81.   The signal box was erected in 1902 and closed in August 1958. The remaining single line is seen in July 1959, by which time a hand-worked point had been installed one mile to the east for the Presteign branch, eliminating the double track section. (H.C.Casserley)

82.   The station water supply had been upgraded somewhat by June 1961, milk tankers generally being glass lined, but drinking water still arrived by train in churns. The goods yard was officially in use until line closure on 28th September 1964. (R.G.Nelson/T.Walsh)

83.   The property was purchased by a retired railwayman and track laying southward started in the 1980s. About one mile was complete by 2007 and some steam trips were run from August 2005 using Peckett no. 1738. The site is private, but self catering holidays can be enjoyed in an ex-LMS coach. There was a rare open day on 14th July 2007, when 0-6-0PT no. 6430 visited the "Kingfisher Line", so called because of the resident birds and the boot polish using that trade name, made adjacent to the goods yard during World War II. (Mrs L.Hunt)

KINGTON

XXI. The 1928 map has the 1857 line from Leominster top right and the 1875 track to New Radnor on the left. It is clear that this was on a different alignment to the final length of the original branch, the terminal area of which became an enlarged goods yard. The engine shed is on the left, as is a narrow gauge railway used by the gasworks. The population fell from 2668 in 1901 to 1880 in 1961.

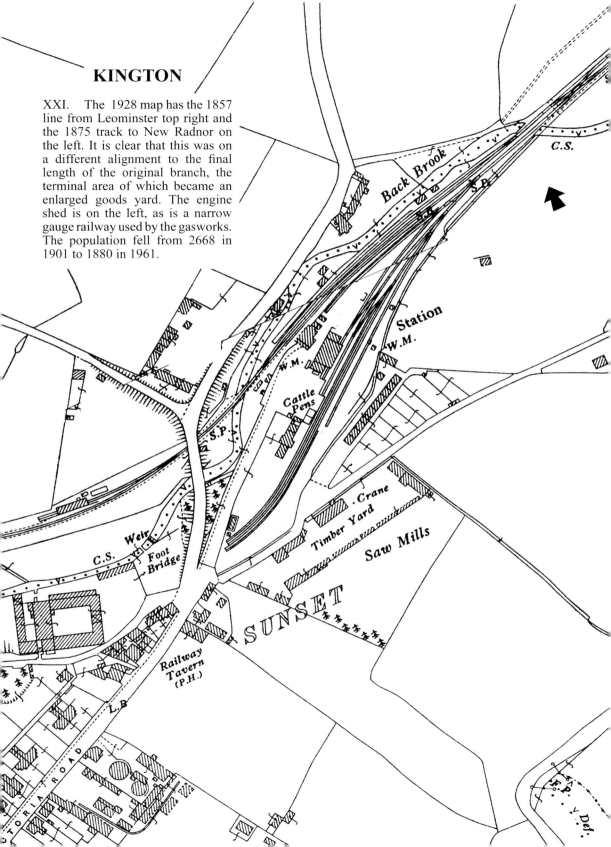

Back Brook

C.S.

S.P.

Station *W.M.*

W.M.

Cattle Pens

S.P.

Crane

Timber Yard

Saw Mills

C.S. *Weir*

Foot Bridge

SUNSET

Railway Tavern (P.H.)

L.B.

VICTORIA ROAD

F.P.

v Def.

84. The annual sale of over 20,000 sheep in the town on one day each August generated massive traffic. One report in 1938 listed a 2.0pm departure of 30 wagons, 60 leaving near 4.0pm and the 6.0pm train being ¼ mile long. An amazing 200 wagons would be in readiness for loading. (GWR)

85. The 1875 station had two lengthy platforms, both often being occupied simultaneously. This is a 1954 view towards New Radnor and it shows the 1904 platform extension on the right. (Stations UK)

86.   A panorama from the road bridge in 1954 looks over the bridge over the brook to the spacious approach area to the station and goods shed. There was a staff of 19 in 1903 and the late 1930s, but it dropped to 13 in 1931, during the Depression. (Stations UK)

87.   A view in the opposite direction in 1957 shows the foot crossing again and the bracket signal more clearly. Below it is the weighbridge office. The B4355 was carried over the railway on Sunset Bridge, which was named after the locality. (R.M.Casserley)

88.   The end of the original line is in view in July 1957, together with one of the platforms. It was mainly used for goods and also for sheep, as seen. (R.M.Casserley)

89.   The original passenger platform and building was also photographed in 1957. We are looking over the cattle pens towards the goods shed. (J.Langford)

90.   The final 1957 view includes the down water column, the unsurfaced foot crossing which had been for passenger use and the 1904 signal box. It was in use until August 1958 and had 37 levers. (R.M.Casserley)

91.   This is a 1959 view of the 1875 passenger station. It is the year after it had closed and the whole site had been given over to goods. The sign refers to Lever's Store. On the right is a Commer lorry and centre is a Thornycroft. (H.C.Casserley)

Kington	1903	1913	1923	1933
Passenger tickets issued	28300	23800	19468	6954
Season tickets issued	*	*	45	2
Parcels forwarded	15695	17864	17457	16188
General goods forwarded (tons)	1171	1532	1433	1009
Coal and coke received (tons)	1905	1686	892	1259
Other minerals received (tons)	1515	1663	628	596
General goods received (tons)	4532	4781	5387	6013
Trucks of livestock handled	517	371	601	609
(* not available)				

92.   The view from the road bridge in 1961 was dominated by the new warehouse for agricultural goods, but all the older buildings remained. The coach body was another late addition, it replacing an earlier one. (J.Langford)

93.   A June 1961 photograph has the original station beyond the goods shed and the second one beyond the coal wagons. Its platforms are on the right, as are one of the water columns and the tank. (R.G.Nelson/T.Walsh)

94.   Our final view of this rural outpost includes the goods shed and original station, shortly before line closure in 1964. No. 1420 is about to leave for Leominster with a train of appeal to a railway modeller. (D.Wilson)

WEST OF KINGTON

95.   Two locomotives and three crews were based here between the wars. Only one engine was needed after 1940 and the shed closed on 5th February 1951. (A.Dudman coll.)

96.   About one mile from Kington was this crossing, called Flood Gates. We are looking west as closure took place. Our journey would soon pass into Wales near here. (H.C.Casserley)

STANNER

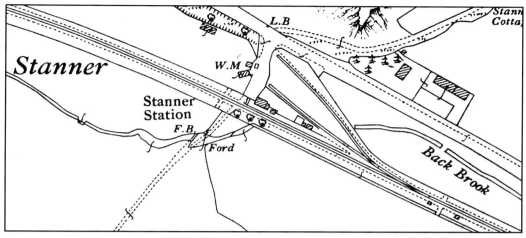

Stanner	1903	1913	1923	1933
Passenger tickets issued	3046	3186	2904	1083
Season tickets issued	*	*	-	2
Parcels forwarded	1215	1786	650	716
General goods forwarded (tons)	110	211	439	845
Coal and coke received (tons)	536	918	599	1848
Other minerals received (tons)	97	92	106	213
General goods received (tons)	252	219	140	94
Trucks of livestock handled	22	20	19	18
(* not available)				

XXII. The 1928 map has the A44 running parallel to the railway. The village residents numbered 161 in 1901. The northern siding had been added in 1928.

97.   A view from August 1932 includes most of the goods yard, where Walter Morgan was coal merchant for many years. The nearest structure is the lamp room. (Mowat coll./Brunel University)

98.   Another picture from the 1930s and this includes the tiny goods shed (left) and the hut for the ground frame, in the distance. The goods yard was open until 9th June 1958. (Lens of Sutton coll.)

99.   There had been two men on duty here usually, but staffing ceased on 28th July 1941, when halt status was bestowed. This 1954 photograph shows that no such additional nameboard was provided. (Stations UK)

DOLYHIR

XXIII. The 1928 survey shows the extent of the limestone quarries here,
together with the numerous limekilns.

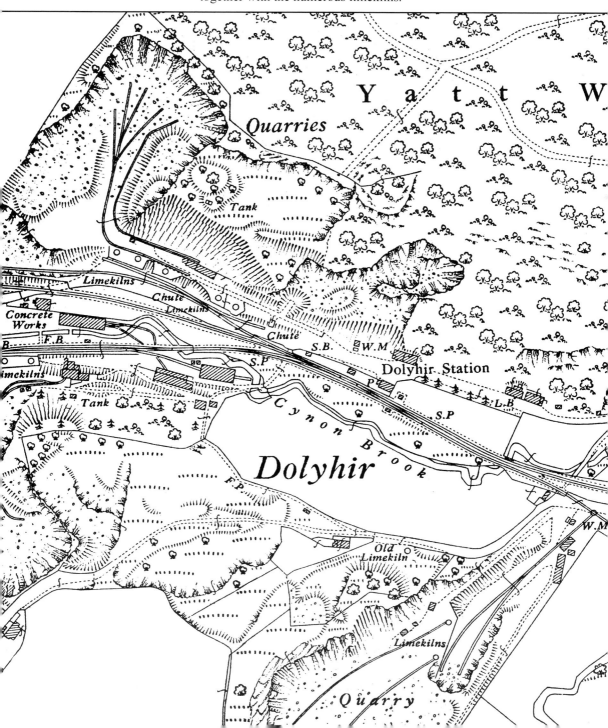

100.   The local population comprised 162 souls in 1901 and the staff numbered one in 1903. However, three was the usual number from 1913 onwards. The plant vases on the platform were made in the adjacent quarry from "Granitic", a form of concrete. (R.S.Carpenter coll.)

Dolyhir	1903	1913	1923	1933
Passenger tickets issued	5059	4927	3994	1986
Season tickets issued	*	*	-	-
Parcels forwarded	560	1641	656	395
General goods forwarded (tons)	70	162	65	841
Coal and coke received (tons)	1594	1694	2149	712
Other minerals received (tons)	83	26	80	36
General goods received (tons)	177	304	463	226
Trucks of livestock handled	-	-	-	-
(* not available)				

101.   The ground frame was in the nearest building, it having five levers. Most of the loop and the original low platform can be seen in this eastward view from 1954. (Stations UK)

102.   Another 1954 picture looks toward the North Kilns, which were initially operated by the Old Radnor Trading Company, as were South Kilns. Those behind the camera were latterly run by the Nash Rocks, Stone & Lime Company. (Stations UK)

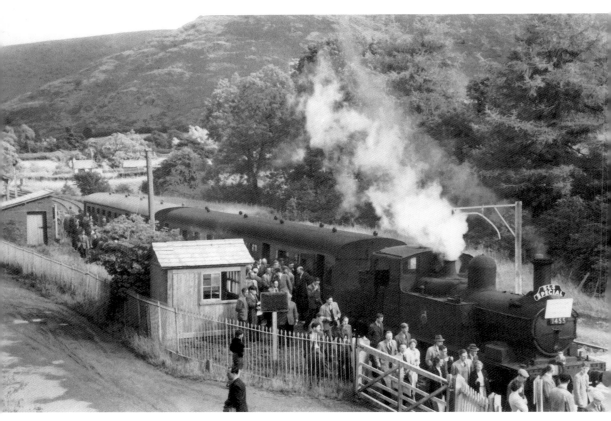

103. The first passengers since 1951 arrived on 27th July 1957 and formed the largest crowd ever on this remote platform. Freight operation ceased here on 9th June 1958, but no trains had run west hereof after 1951. (H.B.Priestley/P.Q.Treloar coll.)

NEW RADNOR

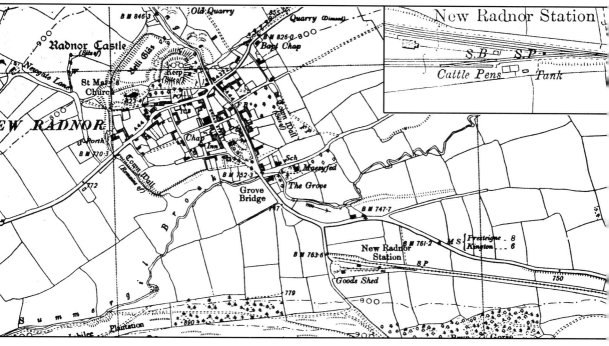

New Radnor	1903	1913	1923	1933
Passenger tickets issued	4716	4217	4083	1355
Season tickets issued	*	*	4	-
Parcels forwarded	2884	3980	4054	2578
General goods forwarded (tons)	451	114	147	204
Coal and coke received (tons)	420	520	356	346
Other minerals received (tons)	127	57	194	108
General goods received (tons)	677	597	447	936
Trucks of livestock handled	119	98	36	31
(* not available)				

XXIV. The 1953 edition at 6ins to 1 mile shows the isolated location of the station. One siding was extended across the road for Caswell & Bowden in 1894. It had once been an important assize town, but population was down to 405 in 1901 and 321 in 1961. The insert is from 1903.

104. The station was recorded in its prime in the 1920s, on a postcard. A single platform sufficed and there was a staff of one from 1929 onwards. (Lens of Sutton coll.)

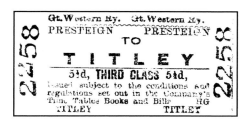

←———— 105. Another postcard presented a rare busy scene from the early 20th century. In the centre is a wooden platform which facilitated the loading of carts and traps, also the unloading of milk churns. (Lens of Sutton coll.)

106.   Few termini had such limited facilities. Ex-GWR 0-6-0PT no. 5765 waits to depart with the 6.5pm to Presteign on 15th September 1949. Passenger service was withdrawn on 5th February 1951. (T.J.Edgington)

107.   Goods traffic ceased on 31st December 1951 and the remains were photographed in 1954. The loop remained in a straight line with the track eastwards, as evidence of the original intention to take the railway further into Wales. (Stations UK)

108.   The only view we have of the goods shed is from 1961, when only sheep visited the scene regularly. This must have been one of the most uneconomic stations on the GWR system. The area became a caravan park. (J.Langford)

3. Presteign Branch

FORGE CROSSING HALT

109.   A 1954 southward view hints at the minimal provision on offer. The halt was added on 9th March 1929. (J.Peden/Stations UK)

110.   By June 1964, nature had full use of the platform, the service having been withdrawn on 5th February 1951. The branch was steeply graded and very undulating. (P.J.Garland/R.S.Carpenter coll.)

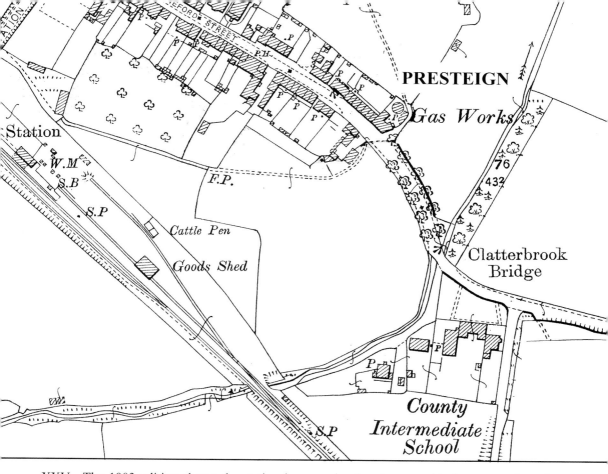

XXV. The 1903 edition shows the station in an undeveloped area, with the approach tracks spanning the Clatter Brook. The first station was thought to be south of the school.

111.   The first terminus opened on 10th September 1875. The second is seen in 1925 with 2021 class 0-6-0ST no. 2153, plus two four-wheeled coaches. The station was about 500ft above sea level. (Lens of Sutton coll.)

112.   This 1932 photograph gives a comprehensive view of the facilities, which differ little from the plan, except for the addition of the short siding in the foreground. One of the two signals is near the goods shed; both were lost and the box was closed in about 1940.
(Mowat coll./Brunel University)

Presteign	1903	1913	1923	1933
Passenger tickets issued	9842	8145	6162	2701
Season tickets issued	*	*	-	-
Parcels forwarded	11614	11013	10354	9370
General goods forwarded (tons)	2345	3624	981	1838
Coal and coke received (tons)	1607	1789	913	901
Other minerals received (tons)	1877	2993	3306	207
General goods received (tons)	2433	2743	2080	1351
Trucks of livestock handled	164	131	225	113

(* not available)

113.   The platform canopy was lost in about 1950 and passenger trains were withdrawn on 5th February 1951, the same day as withdrawal at New Radnor. On the left of this 1954 view is the weighbridge office. (Stations UK)

114.   The SLS railtour of 27th July 1957 was the only train to carry passengers during the final 13 years of the branch. The exception to the rule is visible; the name has a third "e", to comply with local custom. A second photograph of the visit follows. (R.M.Casserley)

115.   As students make a thorough examination of every facet of the premises, we can study the end and side loading dock, which was added in about 1904. Also worthy of note is the lamp room. (R.M.Casserley)

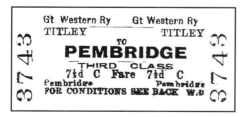

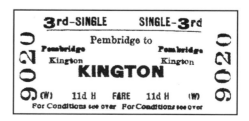

116.   The building had one room in use as a goods office and is seen in July 1959. The population of the town fell from 1910 in 1871 to 1190 in 1961 and it ceased to be a county town in 1974. (R.M.Casserley)

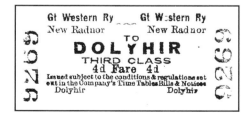

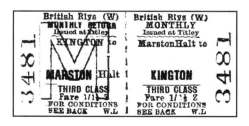

117.   In the final years, the van on the left was used as an office, while traffic diminished. This is the scene on 29th June 1961. There was a one-ton crane in the goods shed. (R.G.Nelson/T.Walsh)

118.   Moving down the yard on the same day, we see the remnants of the once important cattle dock on the left. There had been a staff of three at the station in the period 1929-39. (R.G.Nelson/T.Walsh)

←————— 119.   One of the most productive parts of this "branch of a branch" was the allotment area. Many loco crews were involved in distribution networks, sometimes shooting game on the journey. (R.G.Nelson/T.Walsh)

120.   In the final Summer, there was a last burst of activity and no. 1420 was involved with delivery of material for a gas pipeline. Total closure of both remaining branches came on 28th September 1964 and life was extinguished from these charming rural byways for ever. (D.Wilson)

Middleton Press
EVOLVING THE ULTIMATE RAIL ENCYCLOPEDIA

Easebourne Lane, Midhurst, West Sussex.
GU29 9AZ Tel:01730 813169
www.middletonpress.co.uk email:info@middletonpress.co.uk

A-978 0 906520 B- 978 1 873793 C- 978 1 901706 D-978 1 904474 E - 978 1 906008

OOP Out of print at time of printing - Please check availability BROCHURE AVAILABLE SHOWING NEW TITLES

A
Abergavenny to Merthyr C 91 8
Abertillery and Ebbw Vale Lines D 84 5
Aldgate & Stepney Tramways B 70 1
Allhallows - Branch Line to A 62 8
Alton - Branch Lines to A 11 6
Andover to Southampton A 82 6
Ascot - Branch Lines around A 64 2
Ashburton - Branch Line to B 95 4
Ashford - Steam to Eurostar B 67 1
Ashford to Dover A 48 2
Austrian Narrow Gauge D 04 3
Avonmouth - BL around D 42 5
Aylesbury to Rugby D 91 3
B
Baker Street to Uxbridge D 90 6
Banbury to Birmingham D 27 2
Barking to Southend C 80 2
Barnet & Finchley Tramways B 93 0
Barry - Branch Lines around D 50 0
Basingstoke to Salisbury A 89 5
Bath Green Park to Bristol C 36 9
Bath to Evercreech Junction A 60 4
Bath Tramways B 86 2
Battle over Portsmouth 1940 A 29 1
Battle over Sussex 1940 A 79 6
Bedford to Wellingborough D 31 9
Betwixt Petersfield & Midhurst A 94 9
Bletchley to Cambridge D 94 4
Bletchley to Rugby E 07 9
Blitz over Sussex 1941-42 B 35 0
Bodmin - Branch Lines around B 83 1
Bognor at War 1939-45 B 59 6
Bombers over Sussex 1943-45 B 51 0
Bournemouth & Poole Trys B 47 3
Bournemouth to Evercreech Jn A 46 8
Bournemouth to Weymouth A 57 4 OOP
Bournemouth Trolleybuses C 10 9
Bradford Trolleybuses D 19 7
Brecon to Neath D 43 2
Brecon to Newport D 16 6
Brecon to Newtown E 06 2
Brickmaking in Sussex B 19 6 OOP
Brightons Tramways B 02 2 OOP
Brighton to Eastbourne A 16 1
Brighton to Worthing A 03 1
Brighton Trolleybuses D 34 0
Bristols Tramways B 57 2
Bristol to Taunton D 03 6
Bromley South to Rochester B 23 7
Bromsgrove to Birmingham D 87 6
Bromsgrove to Gloucester D 73 9
Brunel - A railtour of his achievements D 74 6
Bude - Branch Line to B 29 9
Burnham to Evercreech Jn A 68 0
Burton & Ashby Tramways C 51 2
C
Camberwell & West Norwood Tys B 22 0
Cambridge to Ely D 55 5
Canterbury - Branch Lines around B 58 9
Cardiff Trolleybuses D 64 7
Caterham & Tattenham Corner B 25 1
Changing Midhurst C 15 4
Chard and Yeovil - BLs around C 30 7
Charing Cross to Dartford A 75 8
Charing Cross to Orpington A 96 3
Cheddar - Branch Line to B 90 9
Cheltenham to Andover C 43 7
Cheltenham to Redditch D 81 4
Chesterfield Tramways D 37 1
Chesterfield Trolleybuses D 51 7
Chester Tramways E 04 8
Chichester to Portsmouth A 14 7
Clapham & Streatham Trys B 97 8
Clapham Junction - 50 yrs C 06 2 OOP
Clapham Junction to Beckenham Jn B 36 7
Cleobury Mortimer - Branch Lines around E 18 5
Clevedon & Portishead - BLs to D 18 0
Collectors Trains, Trolleys & Trams D 29 6
Colonel Stephens D62 3
Cornwall Narrow Gauge D 56 2
Cowdray & Easebourne D 96 8
Crawley to Littlehampton A 34 5
Cromer - Branch Lines around C 26 6
Croydons Tramways B 42 8
Croydons Trolleybuses B 73 2 OOP
Croydon to East Grinstead B 48 0
Crystal Palace (HL) & Catford Loop A 87 1
Cyprus Narrow Gauge E13 0
D
Darlington to Newcastle D 98 2
Darlington Trolleybuses D 33 3
Dartford to Sittingbourne B 34 3
Derby Tramways D 17 3
Derby Trolleybuses C 72 7
Derwent Valley - Branch Line to the D 06 7
Devon Narrow Gauge E 09 3
Didcot to Banbury D 02 9
Didcot to Swindon C 84 0
Didcot to Winchester C 13 0
Dorset & Somerset Narrow Gauge D 76 0
Douglas to Peel C 88 8
Douglas to Port Erin C 55 0
Douglas to Ramsey D 39 5
Dovers Tramways B 24 4
Dover to Ramsgate A 78 9
E
Ealing to Slough C 42 0
Eastbourne to Hastings A 27 7 OOP
East Cornwall Mineral Railways D 22 7
East Croydon to Three Bridges A 53 6
East Grinstead - Branch Lines to A 07 9
East Ham & West Ham Tramways B 52 7
East Kent Light Railway A 61 1 OOP
East London - Branch Lines of C 44 4
East London Line B 80 0
East Ridings Secret Resistance D 21 0
Edgware & Willesden Tramways C 18 5
Effingham Junction - BLs around A 74 1
Eltham & Woolwich Tramways B 74 9 OOP
Ely to Kings Lynn C 53 6
Ely to Norwich C 90 1
Embankment & Waterloo Tramways B 41 1
Enfield & Wood Green Trys C 03 1 OOP
Enfield Town & Palace Gates - BL to D 32 6
Epsom to Horsham A 30 7
Euston to Harrow & Wealdstone C 89 5
Exeter & Taunton Tramways B 32 9
Exeter to Barnstaple B 15 2
Exeter to Newton Abbot C 49 9
Exeter to Tavistock B 69 5
Exmouth - Branch Lines to B 00 8
F
Fairford - Branch Line to A 52 9
Falmouth, Helston & St. Ives - BL to C 74 1
Fareham to Salisbury A 67 3
Faversham to Dover B 05 3
Felixstowe & Aldeburgh - BL to D 20 3
Fenchurch Street to Barking C 20 8
Festiniog - 50 yrs of enterprise C 83 3
Festiniog 1946-55 E 01 7 - PUB 21 APRIL
Festiniog in the Fifties B 68 8
Festiniog in the Sixties B 91 6
Finsbury Park to Alexandra Palace C 02 4
Frome to Bristol B 77 0
Fulwell - Trams, Trolleys & Buses D 11 1
G
Gloucester to Bristol D 35 7
Gloucester to Cardiff D 66 1
Gosport & Horndean Trys B 92 3
Gosport - Branch Lines around A 36 9
Great Yarmouth Tramways D 13 5
Greece Narrow Gauge D 72 2
Greenwich & Dartford Tramways B 14 5 OOP
Grimsby & Cleethorpes Trolleybuses D 86 9
Guildford to Redhill A 63 5 OOP
H
Hammersmith & Hounslow Trys C 33 8
Hampshire Narrow Gauge D 36 4
Hampshire Waterways A 84 0 OOP
Hampstead & Highgate Tramways B 53 4
Harrow to Watford D 14 2
Hastings to Ashford A 37 6
Hastings Tramways B 18 3
Hastings Trolleybuses B 81 7 OOP
Hawkhurst - Branch Line to A 66 6
Hay-on-Wye - Branch Lines around D 92 0
Hayling - Branch Line to A 12 3
Haywards Heath to Seaford A 28 4
Hemel Hempstead - Branch Lines to D 88 3
Henley, Windsor & Marlow - BL to C77 2
Hereford to Newport D 54 8
Hexham to Carlisle D 75 3
Hitchin to Peterborough D 07 4
Holborn & Finsbury Tramways B 79 4
Holborn Viaduct to Lewisham A 81 9
Horsham - Branch Lines to A 02 4
Huddersfield Tramways D 95 1
Huddersfield Trolleybuses C 92 5
Hull Tramways D60 9
Hull Trolleybuses D 24 1
Huntingdon - Branch Lines around A 93 2
I
Ilford & Barking Tramways B 61 9
Ilford to Shenfield C 97 0
Ilfracombe - Branch Line to B 21 3
Ilkeston & Glossop Tramways D 40 1
Industrial Rlys of the South East A 09 3
Ipswich to Saxmundham C 41 3
Ipswich Trolleybuses D 59 3
Isle of Wight Lines - 50 yrs C 12 3
K
Keighley Tramways & Trolleybuses D 83 8
Kent & East Sussex Waterways A 72 X
Kent Narrow Gauge C 45 1
Kent Seaways - Hoys to Hovercraft D 79 1
Kidderminster to Shrewsbury E10 9
Kingsbridge - Branch Line to C 98 7
Kingston & Hounslow Loops A 83 3 OOP
Kingston & Wimbledon Tramways B 56 5
Kingswear - Branch Line to C 17 8
L
Lambourn - Branch Line to C 70 3
Launceston & Princetown - BL to C 19 2
Lewisham & Catford Tramways B 26 8 OOP
Lewisham to Dartford A 92 5
Lines around Wimbledon B 75 6
Liverpool Street to Chingford D 01 2
Liverpool Street to Ilford C 34 5
Liverpool Tramways - Eastern C 04 8
Liverpool Tramways - Northern C 46 8
Liverpool Tramways - Southern C 23 9
Llandudno & Colwyn Bay Tramways E 17 8
London Bridge to Addiscombe B 20 6
London Bridge to East Croydon A 58 1
London Chatham & Dover Railway A 88 8
London Termini - Past and Proposed D 00 5
London to Portsmouth Waterways B 43 5
Longmoor - Branch Lines to A 41 3
Looe - Branch Line to C 22 2
Ludlow to Hereford E 14 7
Lyme Regis - Branch Line to A 45 1
Lynton - Branch Line to B 04 6
M
Maidstone & Chatham Tramways B 40 4
Maidstone Trolleybuses C 00 0 OOP
March - Branch Lines around B 09 1
Margate & Ramsgate Tramways C 52 9
Marylebone to Rickmansworth D49 4
Melton Constable to Yarmouth Beach E 03 1
Midhurst - Branch Lines around A 49 9
Midhurst - Branch Lines to A 01 7 OOP
Military Defence of West Sussex A 23 9
Military Signals, South Coast C 54 3
Minehead - Branch Line to A 80 2
Mitcham Junction Lines B 01 5
Mitchell & company C 59 8
Monmouthshire Eastern Valleys D 71 5
Moreton-in-Marsh to Worcester D 26 5
Moretonhampstead - BL to C 27 7
Mountain Ash to Neath D 80 7
N
Newbury to Westbury C 66 6
Newcastle to Hexham D 69 2
Newcastle Trolleybuses D 78 4
Newport (IOW) - Branch Lines to A 26 0
Newquay - Branch Lines to C 71 0
Newton Abbot to Plymouth C 60 4
Northern France Narrow Gauge C 75 8
North East German Narrow Gauge D 44 9
North Kent Tramways B 44 2
North London Line B 94 7
North Woolwich - BLs around C 65 9
Norwich Tramways C 40 6
Nottinghamshire & Derbyshire T/B D 63 0
Nottinghamshire & Derbyshire T/W D 53 1
O
Ongar - Branch Lines to E 05 5
Orpington to Tonbridge B 03 9 OOP
Oxford to Bletchley D57 9
Oxford to Moreton-in-Marsh D 15 9
P
Paddington to Ealing C 37 6
Paddington to Princes Risborough C 81 9
Padstow - Branch Line to B 54 1
Plymouth - BLs around B 98 5
Plymouth to St. Austell C 63 5
Pontypool to Mountain Ash D 65 4
Porthmadog 1954-94 - BL around B 31 2
Porthmadog to Blaenau B 50 3 OOP
Portmadoc 1923-46 - BL around B 13 8
Portsmouths Tramways B 72 5
Portsmouth to Southampton A 31 4
Portsmouth Trolleybuses C 73 4
Potters Bar to Cambridge D 70 8
Princes Risborough - Branch Lines to D 05 0
Princes Risborough to Banbury C 85 7
R
Railways to Victory C 16 1 OOP
Reading to Basingstoke B 27 5
Reading to Didcot C 79 6
Reading to Guildford A 47 5 OOP
Reading Tramways B 87 9
Reading Trolleybuses C 05 5
Redhill to Ashford A 73 4
Return to Blaenau 1970-82 C 64 2
Rickmansworth to Aylesbury D 61 6
Roman Roads of Hampshire D 67 8
Roman Roads of Kent E 02 4
Roman Roads of Surrey C 61 1
Roman Roads of Sussex C 48 2
Romneyrail C 32 1
Ryde to Ventnor A 19 2
S
Salisbury to Westbury B 39 8
Salisbury to Yeovil B 06 0 OOP
Saxmundham to Yarmouth C 69 7
Saxony Narrow Gauge D 47 0
Scarborough Tramways E 15 4
Seaton & Eastbourne Tramways B 76 3 OOP
Seaton & Sidmouth - Branch Lines to A 95 6
Secret Sussex Resistance B 82 4
SECR Centenary album C 11 6 OOP
Selsey - Branch Line to A 04 8
Sheerness - Branch Lines around B 16 9 OOP
Shepherds Bush to Uxbridge T/Ws C 28 4
Shrewsbury - Branch Line to A 86 4
Sierra Leone Narrow Gauge D 28 9
Sirhowy Valley Line E 12 3
Sittingbourne to Ramsgate A 90 1
Slough to Newbury C 56 7
Solent - Creeks, Crafts & Cargoes D 52 4
Southamptons Tramways B 33 6
Southampton to Bournemouth A 42 0
Southend-on-Sea Tramways B 28 2
Southern France Narrow Gauge C 47 5
Southwark & Deptford Tramways B 38 1
Southwold - Branch Line to A 15 4
South Eastern & Chatham Railways C 08 6
South London Line B 46 6
South London Tramways 1903-33 D 10 4
South London Tramways 1933-52 D 89 0
South Shields Trolleybuses E 11 6
St. Albans to Bedford D 08 1
St. Austell to Penzance C 67 3
St. Pancras to Barking D 68 5
St. Pancras to St. Albans C 78 9
Stamford Hill Tramways B 85 5
Steaming through Cornwall B 30 5 OOP
Steaming through Kent A 13 0 OOP
Steaming through the Isle of Wight A 56 7
Steaming through West Hants A 69 7
Stratford upon avon to Birmingham D 77 7
Stratford upon Avon to Cheltenham C 25 3
Strood to Paddock Wood B 12 1 OOP
Surrey Home Guard C 57 4
Surrey Narrow Gauge C 87 1
Surrey Waterways A 51 2 OOP
Sussex Home Guard C 24 6
Sussex Narrow Gauge C 68 0
Sussex Shipping Sail, Steam & Motor D 23 4 O
Swanley to Ashford B 45 9
Swindon to Bristol C 96 3
Swindon to Gloucester D46 3
Swindon to Newport D 30 2
Swiss Narrow Gauge C 94 9
T
Talyllyn - 50 years C 39 0
Taunton to Barnstaple B 60 2
Taunton to Exeter C 82 6
Tavistock to Plymouth B 88 6
Tees-side Trolleybuses D 58 6
Tenterden - Branch Line to A 21 5
Thanets Tramways B 11 4 OOP
Three Bridges to Brighton A 35 2
Tilbury Loop C 86 4
Tiverton - Branch Lines around C 62 8
Tivetshall to Beccles D 41 8
Tonbridge to Hastings A 44 4
Torrington - Branch Lines to B 37 4
Tunbridge Wells - Branch Lines to A 32 1
Twickenham & Kingston Trys C 35 2
Two-Foot Gauge Survivors C 21 5 OOP
U
Upwell - Branch Line to B 64 0
V
Victoria & Lambeth Tramways B 49 7
Victoria to Bromley South A 98 7
Victoria to East Croydon A 40 6 OOP
Vivarais C 31 4 OOP
Vivarais Revisited E 08 6
W
Walthamstow & Leyton Tramways B 65 7
Waltham Cross & Edmonton Trys C 07 9
Wandsworth & Battersea Tramways B 63 3
Wantage - Branch Line to D 25 8
Wareham to Swanage - 50 yrs D 09 8
War on the Line A 10 9
War on the Line VIDEO + 88 0
Waterloo to Windsor A 54 3
Waterloo to Woking A 38 3
Watford to Leighton Buzzard D 45 6
Wenford Bridge to Fowey C 09 3
Westbury to Bath B 55 8
Westbury to Taunton C 76 5
West Cornwall Mineral Railways D 48 7
West Croydon to Epsom B 08 4
West German Narrow Gauge D 93 7
West London - Branch Lines of C 50 5
West London Line B 84 8
West Sussex Waterways A 24 6 OOP
West Wiltshire - Branch Lines of D 12 8
Weymouth - Branch Lines around A 65 9
Willesden Junction to Richmond B 71 8
Wimbledon to Beckenham C 58 1
Wimbledon to Epsom B 62 6
Wimborne - Branch Lines around A 97 0
Wisbech - Branch Lines around C 01 7
Wisbech 1800-1901 C 93 2
Woking to Alton A 59 8
Woking to Portsmouth A 25 3
Woking to Southampton A 55 0
Wolverhampton Trolleybuses D 85 2
Woolwich & Dartford Trolleys B 66 4
Worcester to Birmingham D 97 5
Worcester to Hereford D 38 8
Worthing to Chichester A 06 2
Y
Yeovil - 50 yrs change C 38 3
Yeovil to Dorchester A 76 5 OOP
Yeovil to Exeter A 91 8
York Tramways & Trolleybuses D 82 1